SHOOTING ★STARS★

SHOOTING ★ STARS ★

From the Lens of George Kalinsky

Text by Bart Davis

Foreword by Senator Bill Bradley

SIMON & SCHUSTER

NEW YORK LONDON TORONTO SYDNEY TOKYO SINGAPORE

SIMON & SCHUSTER
Simon & Schuster Building
Rockefeller Center
1230 Avenue of the Americas
New York, New York 10020

Designed by Joel Avirom
Design Assistant: Jim Cozza

Manufactured in the United States of America

10   9   8   7   6   5   4   3   2   1

Library of Congress Cataloging-in-Publication Data is available.

ISBN 0-671-75981-7

To my wife, Ellen,
for her love and the dreams we share.

★

ACKNOWLEDGMENTS

*T*his book is a tribute to the many creative associates and skilled performers who I have had the privilege to photograph and work with over the past twenty-five years. I am indebted to them for their friendship, graciousness, and loyalty.

While the creation of this book was a team effort by many people, I am especially grateful to Jerry Sherman, a very special man who had the vision and determination to make this book a reality.

To Senator Bill Bradley, whose understanding, compassion, and friendship has been greatly appreciated. Thank you for your kind words in the Foreword.

To Bob Gutkowski who inspires creativity and a love of the Garden.

To Monie Begley for her warmth, guidance, and enthusiasm for this book.

To Ken Munoz for his counsel and support on this project.

To the many talented people who gave so much of their valuable time, advice, research, and for sharing their memories of Madison Square Garden history: John Cirillo, Dennis D'Agostino, Tim Donovan, Bobby Goldwater, Steve Griffith, John Halligan, Tommy Kenville, Harry Markson, John Urban, and Chris Weiller.

To Betsy Becker for endless hours of coordinating and research.

To my talented editors, Stuart Gottesman and Jeff Neuman, who are the very best in the business. Stuart deserves special gratitude for navigating this project with patience and care.

To Bart Davis who creates magic with words.

To Dr. Irving Glick and Herb Schwartzman who are always in my corner.

To my friends at the Olympus Camera Corporation who have made me part of their family and whose equipment was used to take most of the photos in these pages.

To everyone at Madison Square Garden and Paramount Communications who has provided leadership and support throughout my career. Your warmth and loyalty have been a positive influence in my life, and have made me feel like a part of the company's rich tradition.

And to my wonderful family who give me encouragement and love; my wife, Ellen, our children, Lee, Rachelle, Larry, and our mothers, Fay and Sadye, who gave us the gift of life.

I love you all,
George Kalinsky,
New York, 1992

CONTENTS

FOREWORD BY SENATOR BILL BRADLEY

George Kalinsky is the most likable and least threatening photographer I've met either as a New York Knick or as a U.S. senator. He is a gentle man with a sensitive eye and a dogged determination to get the perfect shot. As the official photographer of Madison Square Garden for twenty-five years, he has had a unique vantage point from which to shoot the most famous sports and entertainment figures in the world. Personalities such as Muhammad Ali, Peggy Fleming, Bill Russell, Judith Jamison, LeRoy Neiman, Frank Sinatra, and Luciano Pavarotti will all tell you that George has taken their favorite picture.

The photos in this book show hard-fought victory and crushing defeat—the great moments and the not-so-great moments at center ring, at center court, and behind the scenes in "the world's most famous arena." George captures the performers when subject and circumstance join to move us deeply. On my office wall hang two of those special times for me: the exact moments the New York Knicks won the world championships in 1970 and 1973.

Bill Bradley and Willis Reed celebrating the Knicks' 1973 NBA championship.

Since arena performances and spectator sports are two of America's few common enthusiasms, George Kalinsky has recorded moments of our common social history: a dedicated Willis Reed walking out on one good leg to help the Knicks win the NBA championship; a fading Judy Garland drawing strength from an audience chanting, "Judy . . . Judy—we love you"; Muhammad Ali and Joe Frazier giving each other their best for a crowd that came to see and be seen; Luciano Pavarotti performing for the first time off the operatic stage to electrifying encore after encore; a Hoboken singer named Sinatra making each cheering fan feel special; the ever-changing face of Elton John; a silhouetted Billy Joel playing at his piano, and the hands of his fans reaching out to touch him; the memories of great, now-departed performers such as Bing Crosby, Sammy Davis, Jr., Janis Joplin, Jimi Hendrix, Jim Morrison, and, in his final stage performance, John Lennon.

George presents the artists of motion—Earl Monroe, Michael Jordan, Dr. J, Peggy Fleming, Olga Korbut, and so many others from the sports that have graced the Garden with balletlike movements. It is a young Wilt Chamberlain dominating his game and an older Wilt saying good-bye for the very last time. It is hockey and boxing and track and basketball and ice skating. It is Otto Griebling—the circus world's sad and silent clown who gave his last performance and final moment of life before George's camera lens. It is the birth of animals, extravagant weddings, and gala parties. It is presidents and kings and queens. And it is Big Bird and Mickey Mouse.

Finally, it is the audience who formed a central part of the Garden experience. Celebrities, of course: Barbra Streisand, Dustin Hoffman, Neil Simon, Woody Allen, Spike Lee, Michael Douglas, Peter Falk, Bill Cosby, and so many others. But it is more the people who come to the Garden expecting the best, their faces, their hands, their sweat and passion reflecting the performers' own, their sense that there is a link between them and those of us who performed, one that is valuable and intimate and good, one that George Kalinsky has recorded uniquely and dramatically for all time, through his lens.

*I*NTRODUCTION

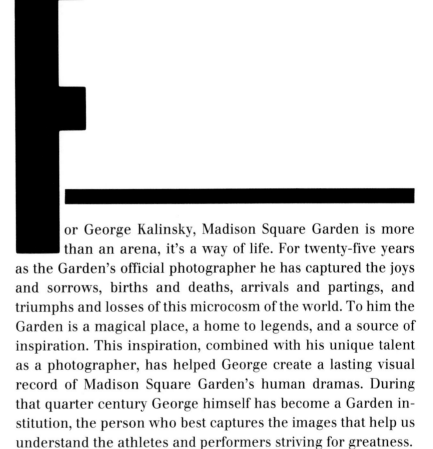

For George Kalinsky, Madison Square Garden is more than an arena, it's a way of life. For twenty-five years as the Garden's official photographer he has captured the joys and sorrows, births and deaths, arrivals and partings, and triumphs and losses of this microcosm of the world. To him the Garden is a magical place, a home to legends, and a source of inspiration. This inspiration, combined with his unique talent as a photographer, has helped George create a lasting visual record of Madison Square Garden's human dramas. During that quarter century George himself has become a Garden institution, the person who best captures the images that help us understand the athletes and performers striving for greatness.

George Kalinsky's fans are numerous. Star after star will tell you he took his or her favorite picture. "George is a true artist. No one can capture the intense emotion of sport like he does," said Willis Reed. Frank Sinatra offers his praise as neatly as he does a lyric: "As a photographer," he says, "Kalinsky is the champ."

Over the years George has developed a special understanding of the Garden. He knows its moves. "For twenty-five years

George has been as important a part of the Garden family as the performers and athletes," said Marv Albert warmly. "His personal presence and the lasting values of his photos have made him the best at what he does." Lasting values. They're what link George and the Garden. Now in its fourth incarnation, Madison Square Garden has presented more than a hundred years of events and performers. The Mecca of Sports and Entertainment, they call it. The House of Champions. The fans appreciate that history. They know the Garden has always been devoted to them, especially the young people. Thirty years ago, General Organization cards got students a half-price admission. That policy is back, which only goes to show that like the Garden itself, good ideas have long lives.

The Old Garden, actually the third Garden, formally opened on December 15, 1925. It said sports the moment you walked in. It was originally constructed for boxing, and the visual focal point was the ring. There was a closeness about the arena, partly because of its vertical construction, a kind of roofed Ebbets Field. The press box overhung the players' bench, and during games, if a player yelled, you could hear *exactly* what was said. You always felt you were in the game, no matter where you sat. You saw the same vendors year after year. There was continuity, a link with the past. You could grab something from the Nedick's that fronted the building on the street, or enter through the Garden's historic lobby. At halftime you might well see a player run out for a hot dog. The intimacy and warmth created a tangible aura.

The old Garden's marquee was part of the building's charm and unique appeal.

The vertical design of the old Garden created a special intimacy between the players and fans.

People arriving by limo or taxi were met by a doorman, so every night was like opening night at the theater. They were let out under the unique canopy proclaiming Madison Square Garden's present and future events, with the *q* on the canopy always just a little askew. The regular folks took the AA and E trains to Fiftieth Street, everyone meeting with total informality in New York's one true melting pot. The Garden was for everyone. Five million people a year, rich and poor, young and old, great and small, came to see the events. If there had been a sign-in book in the lobby for celebrities it would be the longest, most prestigious guest book in the world. But it would be unimportant compared to the cultural heritage the Garden bequeathed to *all* the people of New York.

The Rangers were born here, and college and professional basketball as we know it. The Garden raised to epic proportions the exhibition of prizefighting, track and field, tennis, ballet, ice shows, political rallies, the circus for ten weeks every spring, dog shows, horse shows, concerts, and conventions. It was also the scene of arguably two of the greatest extravaganzas in modern times, the birthday party for John F. Kennedy at which Marilyn Monroe stopped the show singing "Happy Birthday," and film producer Mike Todd's 1957 party for *Around the World in 80 Days*.

George Kalinsky came to the Garden in 1966 and began to record its history of now bygone days. His images enshrine the musty old Boxing Department filled with cigar smoke, which smelled like Gleason's gym; the fifth-floor ice rink, called Iceland, where the Rangers practiced; the huge exhibition hall under the Garden, where the circus displayed its menagerie; even the dingy Belvedere Hotel across the street, where the

rodeo and circus performers stayed—including the man who rode his horse straight into the bar one night.

The story of how George became the official Madison Square Garden photographer is a wonderful tale in itself. Like many Garden stories, it's about talent, timing, and the courage to go for it all. While vacationing in Florida, George spotted Muhammad Ali and Howard Cosell walking into the Fifth Street Gym. He went inside, only to be stopped by Ali's trainer, Angelo Dundee. Up to that point George had used his camera only to take pictures of his family or friends. "I asked Angelo for permission to take a few shots and jokingly told him I was the photographer for Madison Square Garden," recalls Kalinsky. "The words just came out of my mouth and I don't know why." Dundee said, "Why not, Mr. Comedian?" George took twelve shots of the champ training, never realizing that a career was beginning.

"That evening, my wife, Ellen, and I heard on the car radio that Ali's next championship fight against Ernie Terrell was being canceled. This was the top story, so we drove to *The Miami Herald* and asked if they were interested in my film. They developed the roll and sent the photos by wire service to papers across the country. I was on a *roll,* so to speak—my first photos of a celebrity and the world got to see them.

"I owe my photography career to John Condon, an elegant man who was president of Madison Square Garden Boxing. Up until that point I was a graphic and industrial designer, and I had been an art director for a New York agency. John Condon was a public relations genius and a deeply sensitive human being. It was because of John that so many other careers started or blossomed. LeRoy Neiman, Don King, and actor Danny Aiello got their starts with John's help. Boxers like Joe Frazier, Muhammad Ali, George Foreman, and many more trusted in John as an adviser and as a father."

George decided to go to New York to show the photos to John. He told him this was the only roll of sports photos he had ever taken in his life. "I explained my art career and my background in design and he seemed genuinely interested," George recalls. "He said my approach to photography was very different from other photographers' and that he liked the emotion and composition in my one roll. On a hunch, he hired me to take photos for the Garden."

George's first assignment for the Garden in 1966 was to photograph middleweight champion Emile Griffith for his title

fight with Dick Tiger. At that time, Emile was best known for his fight with Benny "Kid" Paret, who had died from the forceful blows inflicted by Emile's quick hands. "I met Emile in a gym near the Garden and found him unexpectedly delightful. He was a happy person with a bubbly Virgin Islands accent. He was definitely not menacing. Using my camera for the first time professionally, I photographed Emile as he went through his training routine with his manager, Gil Clancy. One of the first photos I took was Emile doing neck exercises, his face covered with heavy sweat. To this day, it's one of my favorite pictures."

George took enough photos during the session to feed the newspapers every day for a month, which is exactly what happened. He took all kinds of workout shots, posed shots, and even shower shots. John Condon picked fifty different images and selectively sent them to the newspapers and wire services so that several of them appeared in the papers every day, right up until the night of the fight.

When, two years later, in 1968, the Old Garden closed after forty-three years, George was there as the Garden photographer to record it. The six-day bicycle races had gone the way of dance marathons, the Depression, World War II, and the war in Korea. On the night of the last basketball game, the Harlem Magicians were playing the first game of a doubleheader, with the Knicks against the Philadelphia 76ers as the main event, George photographed the evening as a truly moving and historically important moment in Garden history, documenting the final night of one of the greatest courts the game was ever played on.

The Old Garden left a legacy of stories too numerous to repeat, including one about a Garden employee and his fiancée who left a game early to retrieve their coats from his office, only to stumble onto the body of a fan who had died during the game and had been stored there. But one story sums up the character and charm of the Old Garden best: The office of the Garden's highly respected doctor, Dr. Kazuo Yanagisawa, was a haven for his well-known avocations, gin rummy and cigar smoking. Friends swore that they had never seen Yana, as he was called, without playing cards in his hands. One night a hockey player came in needing stitches while Yana, as gruff as a sumo wrestler, was playing gin with his buddies. Undisturbed, he shifted the cards to his left hand, had his nurse hold the wound closed, and sewed it up with his right hand, never

leaving the game or his cigar. Regulars said he was the only man in the world who could stitch, play cards, and smoke at the same time.

The new Garden officially opened on February 11, 1968, and picked up the great traditions of the old as smoothly as Willis Reed scored off a Walt Frazier pass. George was more experienced now, his images stronger. He had developed his unique ability to "telegraph intense emotion and preserve it," as Peggy Fleming put it, and he had realized many of the artistic principles that underlie his work.

The newly renovated Garden is still recognized by its signature ceiling.

"When someone is performing in a sporting event or entertaining, they're going to arrive at certain peak moments. When that moment comes, when the person's emotions are communicated through the *hands,* the *eyes,* and the *mouth,* that's the time to take the picture. I'm not overly concerned with an athlete making a great shot. I'm more concerned with an athlete showing feeling. For the most part, that's true with any subject I photograph, and why I'm so drawn to faces."

The magic is when these elements combine to give us pure emotion, a window into the deepest parts of the person. "George Kalinsky captures the art and spiritual essence of athletes, performers, and other public figures better than any pho-

tographer I have ever seen," said *New York Times* columnist George Vecsey.

George drives himself to find the enduring images in every single event, from the NBA play-offs to the dog show. No matter what the event, his photos "vibrate with that special energy when photojournalism becomes art," said Jack Kroll of *Newsweek.* "Kalinsky always captures the hot moment." To do that, George becomes part of the communication between the performers and the audience, relating to all its aspects as he selects moments that will often be viewed for years to come.

Of all the events at the Garden, few match the electricity of a championship fight, or offer greater challenges and rewards to a photographer. The sixty-six-year-old Madison Square Garden boxing ring canvas is where the champions have stood: Joe Louis, Ali and Frazier, Graziano, Patterson, Robinson, and so many others. One hundred sixty championship dramas have been played out on it. No ring anywhere can match that tribute to the will to win by half, or half again.

Just as the Garden boxing ring has been the province of its great champions, many of the Garden's special stages have always been linked to famous stars. The skating rink was for the Queen of the Ice, Sonja Henie; the three rings for the Ringling Brothers circus; the tennis court for Pancho Segura; the track for Glenn Cunningham, six-time winner of the Wanamaker mile; the hockey rink for Bobby Hull and Gordie Howe and Rod Gilbert.

Even now, at the beautifully renovated Garden, there's that same rich sense of history. Look up to the banners draped from the ceiling, enduring tributes to Holzman, Giacomin, Gilbert, Frazier, Barnett, McGuire, Monroe, Reed, DeBusschere, Bradley. Overhead is the signature ceiling that says you're in the

An era of glamour has returned to the Garden with the opening of the new Paramount theater.

Garden. Or sit under the starlit canopy of the new Paramount theater. An era of glamour and glory has come again and one thing is clear: You're in the most famous building in the world, "the most magnificent arena in creation."

George's enduring images of will, drive, and desire explain why we come to this "magnificent arena." He shows us the shared spirit and joy of the audience and the competitors and the performers. We see memories from our past, and hopes for the future. Through George's images we magnify our spirit, amateur warriors linking ourselves to greatness. The majesty of these great men and women is so near we feel we better understand them and all the things they do so well. This is George's unique gift, capturing the truths of performance with his own special artistry.

"I really believe that any prospective photographer should have a foundation in design and composition. Pratt Institute taught me what line, form, and texture are all about. I try and combine these design and form elements to communicate as both an artist and a reporter to tell a story. If caught correctly, the instant lives on as an expression of time. Whether it's the grace and style of Michael Jordan floating towards the basket, or Peggy Fleming skating, or the expression of confidence on the face of Frank Sinatra, I try and freeze these 'emotions in motion' to preserve them in my album of memories. For me, a photo is like a painting, our lives are the palette, my camera is the brush. Pictures that convey deep emotion create a powerful canvas, one that forces us to respond with happiness or anger, for the sake of beauty or despair."

George has had a unique opportunity to be close to performers and athletes. He sees the months and years they spend perfecting their art, their determination and desire to be successes. He sees people who are proud and scared, who cry and laugh; people who are just like us. Armed with his Olympus camera, he covers his beat "with the eye of an artist," said LeRoy Neiman, and always evokes a "winning style." George often meets performers backstage and observes their private moments. He sees personality and character away from the stage, and is able to capture people in a more revealing light. A lot of athletes come into his office to talk, often of very personal matters. He is a good listener, a deeply caring man. Over the years, many deep personal bonds have been formed.

There is always more to George's photographs than just the image. Present in every one of his shots are the dramatic elements of story, a beginning, a middle, and an end. These elements combine before our eyes and capture us, insisting that we will know more about the subject the deeper we look. His images show us that feelings are universal.

"Joe Frazier once told me I captured the peak moment of his life. It was one split second when he hit Ali and both of Joe's feet were off the ground, which made it a punch that he got all he had into. Everything was perfect in that picture. He lived a lifetime for that moment. The photograph was the culmination of his career. That's the most rewarding part of the job, when someone says my photo was the best ever taken of them, or it was an important moment of their life."

For more than twenty-five years at nearly four thousand separate events, George has preserved human emotions so vibrant and clear we instantly recognize them and know we have felt them too. His photographs show us one sure truth: that there *is* a link connecting all of us, one that is valuable and intimate and good, one that George Kalinsky sees and shows us again and again through the lens of his camera.

A WILL TO WIN

Fire in the eyes, clenched fists, hardness in the mouth. These are the visible signs of emotion in sports. Night after night, George Kalinsky moves among coaches and players looking for strong emotions, the intensity that can lead to unforgettable moments of victory and defeat. He watches closely as the players leave for the court, the rink, or the ring. By looking at faces and talking with players, he can see and hear the emotional edge that makes players, teams, and games special.

A quarter century of intense observation has helped George capture some of the most powerful moments in the history of Madison Square Garden. He knows the athletes and the circumstances, and he understands the importance of a game or event. He sees when will, drive, and desire come together and change everything. The joys of victory become sweeter and the frustrations of failure become even more intense.

"It's that extra drive and desire, the inner determination to do the very best you can. When you feel like that, your own character and pride start to

Willis Reed returning to the floor for game seven of the NBA finals, 1970.

emerge, and when that happens you are ready to capture their pride, character, and determination."

George drives himself to make the most of every game. He believes there's something special to be communicated in every event. "I try to know everything about who's playing, who's performing, the background stories, the personalities, the importance of the game, knowing that a record might be broken. That helps me anticipate some of the action. But I always have to be prepared for the unknowns. You just have to be ready."

George's enduring images of will, drive, and desire often focus on the faces of the competitors. Through their faces, he shows us their joy and anger, their elation and pain, and their dedication to doing the best they can.

BOTTOM

George Foreman after knocking out his opponent in his first professional fight, 1969.

TOP RIGHT

Tom Heinsohn, 1973.

BOTTOM RIGHT

John Starks, 1991.

Eamonn Coghlan, 1987.

Wrestlers Ken Patera and
Tony Atlas at Shea Stadium,
1980.

Mike Allison celebrating the
Rangers' victory over the
Islanders to qualify for the
Stanley Cup finals, 1979.

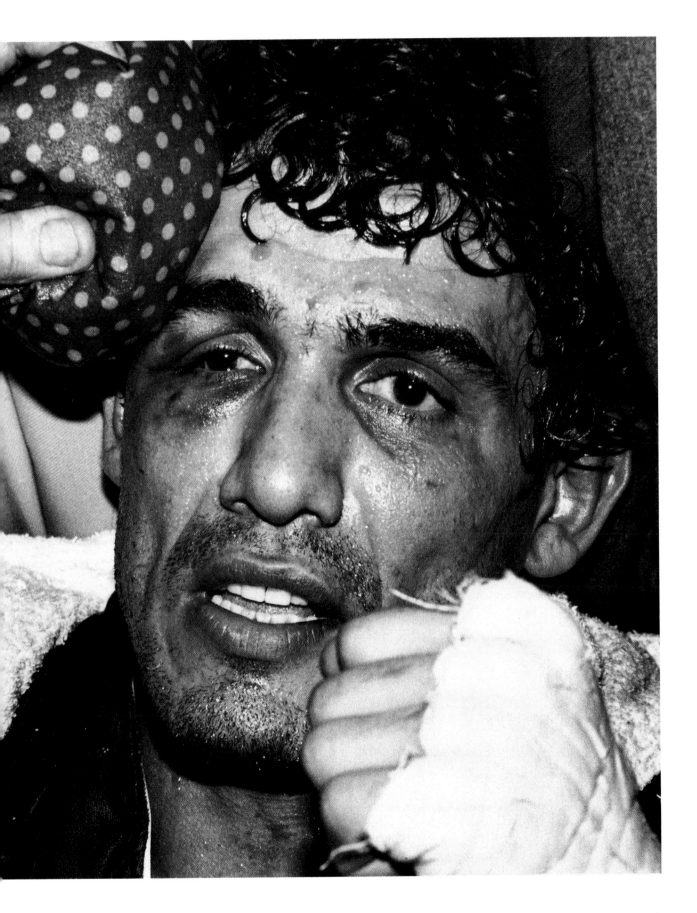

PRECEDING PAGE
Mustafa Hamsho after facing
Marvin Hagler, 1984.

TOP

Dave Maloney after the
Rangers lost to the Islanders in
the Stanley Cup play-offs, 1982.

RIGHT

John McEnroe, 1983.

FOLLOWING PAGE
Muhammad Ali and Joe
Frazier, March 8, 1971.

LEFT

Don Maloney, 1983.

RIGHT

Bobby Hull, 1968.

BOTTOM

Willis Reed lying on the floor in pain after falling in game five of the NBA finals, 1970.

FOLLOWING PAGE

George Chuvalo, 1968.

PRECEDING PAGE

Gilles Villemure, 1970.

LEFT

Sugar Ray Leonard's final bout,
1991.

ABOVE

The Knicks' bench celebrating
during the final seconds of
game seven of the NBA finals,
May 8, 1970.

BEST IN SHOW

TOP LEFT

A two-time Best in Show
champion surrounded by
photographers, 1971.

BOTTOM LEFT

Bob Wolff interviewing the
Best in Show champion at the
Westminster Kennel Club Dog
Show, 1972.

ABOVE

The Westminster Kennel Club
Dog Show, 1971.

LEFT

Lew Alcindor (later Kareem Abdul-Jabbar) playing for UCLA, 1968.

TOP

Amateur gymnast, 1976.

BOTTOM

The Rangers' bench after the team beat the Islanders, 1979.

FOLLOWING PAGE

Joe Frazier defending his heavyweight title against Jerry Quarry. The referee is legendary heavyweight Joe Louis, 1969.

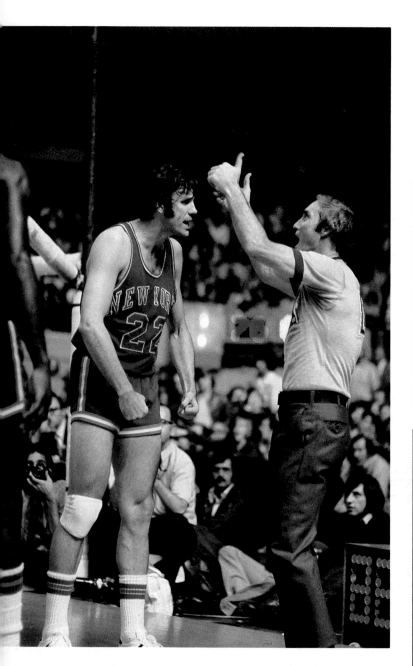

PRECEDING PAGE
Monica Seles, 1990.

LEFT
Dave DeBusschere arguing a
call at the Boston Garden, 1973.

BELOW
The Baltimore Bullets vs. the
New York Knicks, 1967.

RIGHT
Boone Kirkman being counted
out against George Foreman,
1970.

PRECEDING PAGE

The National Horse Show.

BOTTOM LEFT

Pole-vaulter Earl Bell at the
Millrose Games, 1990.

ABOVE RIGHT

Bill Bradley with trainer Danny
Whelan, 1973.

OPPOSITE

Larry Holmes knocks out Mike
Weaver to retain his
heavyweight title, 1979.

THE WORLD
IS A STAGE

Madison Square Garden is a city unto itself, one that never rests. Nowhere but at the Garden, along with the Paramount, will fourteen different events be held on seven consecutive nights, each one exciting and new. There is a laborer, an electrician, or a changeover crew working at every hour of the day or night. The network folks could still be on the air at 3:00 A.M. The building is always awake. There is never total silence.

"The diversity at the Garden is the biggest thrill for me. The variety of performances and performers is always fun because each one poses a different challenge or a different demand. In a very short time I might photograph the circus, a basketball game, and an ice show. Then I go from a dog show to a rock concert to a boxing match. The sheer number of events I've covered amazes me, nearly four thousand. But they all have one thing in common—people. The circus, the ice shows, the press parties, the concerts, they're all about people. People sharing their emotions. My job is uncovering the human element."

Janis Joplin, 1969.

The thrilling diversity of the performances is matched only by the challenges it creates. The goalie's net on the ice for a Rangers game in the afternoon is replaced by a giant stage for a rock concert that night. The next night, spotlights shine on the three rings of a circus. Change is the only constant.

"A photographer shouldn't stand out at any event. I want my pictures to stand out. I try to blend in—that's part of my personality. I dress for the occasion, mostly understated. With all the different staging, I'm very conscious of lighting and positioning, where I'm going to place myself and my equipment. I'm always looking for what the memorable part of the event will be."

One of George's great gifts is his ability to capture the emotions of every subject on every stage. "I want to capture the essence of the evening for people, the most memorable part. I want the picture to be so moving that it will give the viewer the feelings of the performer as well as the record, the full story."

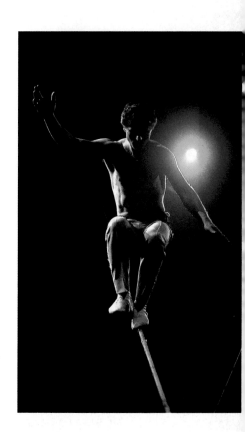

ABOVE

A tightrope walker from the Ringling Brothers and Barnum & Bailey Circus, 1972.

LEFT

"**C**lown of God" performed by the Nijinsky Ballet, 1972.

RIGHT

Bob Hope and Bing Crosby on the opening night of the new Garden, February 11, 1968.

FOLLOWING PAGE

Jimi Hendrix, 1969

PRECEDING PAGE

A tiger in the Ringling Brothers and Barnum & Bailey Circus.

OPPOSITE LEFT

Judy Garland's final American performance, 1968.

LEFT

Thousands of couples being married in a mass ceremony by the Reverend Sun Myung Moon, July 1, 1982.

BELOW

A fire-eater from the Magic and Occult Illusion Show, 1974.

LEFT
Elton John, 1989.

ABOVE
Elephants in the Ringling
Brothers and Barnum & Bailey
Circus, 1991.

RIGHT
Gunther Gebel-Williams, 1981.

FOLLOWING PAGE
Frank Sinatra, 1969.

PRECEDING PAGE
John Lennon's final
performance before his death,
in a guest appearance with
Elton John, 1974.

LEFT
Elvis Presley, 1972.

ABOVE
Paul Simon, 1987.

RIGHT
Juliet Prowse, 1975.

LEFT

Michael Jackson, 1988.

ABOVE

Mickey Mouse on ice in Disney
on Parade, 1970.

RIGHT

Tina Turner, 1987.

LEFT
Mick Jagger, 1975.

ABOVE
Mikhail Baryshnikov and
Judith Jamison, 1976.

RIGHT
Billy Joel, 1986.

NOBODY
DOES IT BETTER

Some performers are simply the best at what they do. Their mastery of their sport is so impressive they seem to outdistance the competition and force us to pay attention. They understand the game, match, or race in a way that no one else ever has before. Suddenly, incredibly complex moves seem effortless and simple craft is elevated to the level of art.

George Kalinsky is constantly trying to capture the artistic beauty of these men and women of motion. "In most cases I'm photographing these great athletes at the height of their career, the peak of their very special skill. I'm always seeing something special; their body shapes and movements become art before my lens. It lifts my level of intensity, too. I'm inspired when I see a Michael Jordan doing what he does better than anyone else."

When Kalinsky photographs superstar athletes, he shifts his focus from the athletes' faces and emotions and emphasizes their body motion. He's out to capture their impeccable timing and precision movement. Ath-

Olga Korbut, 1973.

letes in their prime make moves that are so superb, precise, and poetic that capturing their performances is a record of form at its best. Sometimes, the peak moment can be a non-movement, a stop position. A skater or a gymnast can create a shape that is an art form, a composition of beauty, but only for a split second. It's a remarkable feat to capture that one moment or motion that defines the performer and his or her greatness.

"A big part of what separates these performers from the others is timing. It's a sense of knowing instantly *when*, besides knowing *what*. It's just as critical to the performer as the athlete. Timing for a performer is knowing what to do to get that ultimate audience reaction. For me, timing is being ready to capture that moment when it comes."

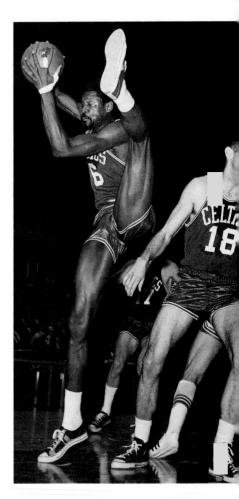

ABOVE RIGHT

Bill Russell in the first basketball game at the new Garden, 1968.

BELOW

Rod Gilbert, 1969.

RIGHT

Jackie Joyner-Kersee, 1988.

LEFT

Pete Maravich playing for LSU, 1968.

ABOVE

John Davidson, 1979.

RIGHT

Dorothy Hamill, 1983.

FOLLOWING PAGE

Jim Ryun posts a 3:57.5 in the "last mile" at the old Garden, 1968.

PRECEDING PAGE
Michael Jordan, 1985.

LEFT
Red Holzman and the Knicks, 1970.

BELOW
Larry Bird, 1990.

RIGHT
Jimmy Connors, 1981.

LEFT
Chris Evert, 1981.

ABOVE
Brian Leetch, 1991.

RIGHT
Walt Frazier and Earl Monroe, 1970.

FOLLOWING PAGE
Wayne Gretzky, 1992.

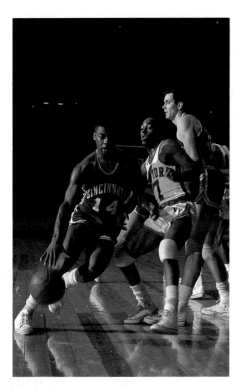

LEFT
Oscar Robertson, 1967.

BELOW
Walt Frazier, 1974.

RIGHT
Martina Navratilova, 1989.

PUBLIC MASKS...

Certain people are so striking, so unique, we feel we know them just by their appearance. Whether they intend it or not, we see their faces, body movements, and costumes, and feel we understand them. What we're seeing and reacting to are their public masks.

Some performers are born wearing their public masks; others carefully craft and refine their images. Billy Joel seems inseparable from his earthy, working-class heroism. But Michael Jackson can shed his public mask and revert to his quiet, private personality as soon as he leaves the stage. Still, both kinds of masks communicate a special essence.

"I try to capture charisma and what makes their personalities unique: costume, facial expression, body movement, and personal style. It's important to notice details. Athletes in their prime strut a certain way, walk a certain way. Performers with that special magnetism, like Sinatra or Burns, actually get better with age. Elton John creates a dazzling mask and visual image through costume, along with his talent. Sinatra doesn't need a costume. His appeal and | **L**uciano Pavarotti, 1984.

stage presence are in his face and hands and the way he moves."

Performers wear masks for power, image, and mystery. When we see their masks, they seem transformed. Their identities always seem fresh, new, and unique. They have an undefinable style. They also share a special love affair with their fans.

"One day, Walt Frazier came into my office in a green suit and a green hat and green alligator shoes," George remembers. "I thought he looked so unusual, so different from his shy, real personality, I decided to take his portrait. I told Walt to come outside and I photographed him leaning against a lamppost. Danny Whelan, the Knicks' trainer, was watching and called him Clyde because he said Walt looked like Clyde from the movie *Bonnie and Clyde.* Frazier loved the idea of playing a character. The photograph appeared in *Newsweek* and other national magazines, and a persona was born."

OPPOSITE LEFT
Michael Jordan, 1991.

LEFT
Gunther Gebel-Williams, 1981.

BELOW
Elvis Presley, 1972.

FOLLOWING PAGE
Hulk Hogan, 1985.

PRECEDING PAGE
Little Richard, 1973.

LEFT
Jim Morrison, 1969.

BELOW
Michael Jackson, 1984.

RIGHT
Otto Griebling, "the world's greatest clown," performing for the last time, 1972.

FOLLOWING PAGE
Red Holzman, 1969.

LEFT

Whoopi Goldberg, New Year's
Eve, 1988.

ABOVE

George Burns, 1989.

RIGHT

Eddie Murphy, 1987.

FOLLOWING PAGE

Promotional art for the Ali–
Frazier fight, 1971.

PRECEDING PAGE
Frank Sinatra, 1974.

LEFT
Patrick Ewing, 1989.

ABOVE
David Bowie, 1976.

RIGHT
John Lennon, 1972.

TRAINING HDQTS.
FOR JOE FRAZIER
HEAVYWEIGHT
CHAMPION

...*PRIVATE FACES*

There is always more to the spectacle than what we see on stage, on the court, or in the rink. There are hours of preparation and powerful emotions. The nervous anxiety of a fighter. The rush of adrenaline as a performer gets ready. Backstage lies halfway between a performer's private life and the public stage. It's where stars sit silently contemplating the perfect performance. It is also where even the greatest artists of sports and the stage are most human, vulnerable, and candid.

Before the action, the dressing room is a sanctuary, a place for privacy. It is also a place to prepare for the public. This is where the plain become pretty, the beautiful glorious. Coaches chew out players, or urge them on to victory. Champagne can flow one night, tears the next. Prayers are said here. Presidents call to offer congratulations. Trainers tape wrists and ankles, patch wounds and stitch faces. Makeup artists create illusion. Costume designers create art.

"I look for concentration behind the scenes. Some people | **M**uhammad Ali at Joe Frazier's gym in Philadelphia, 1971.

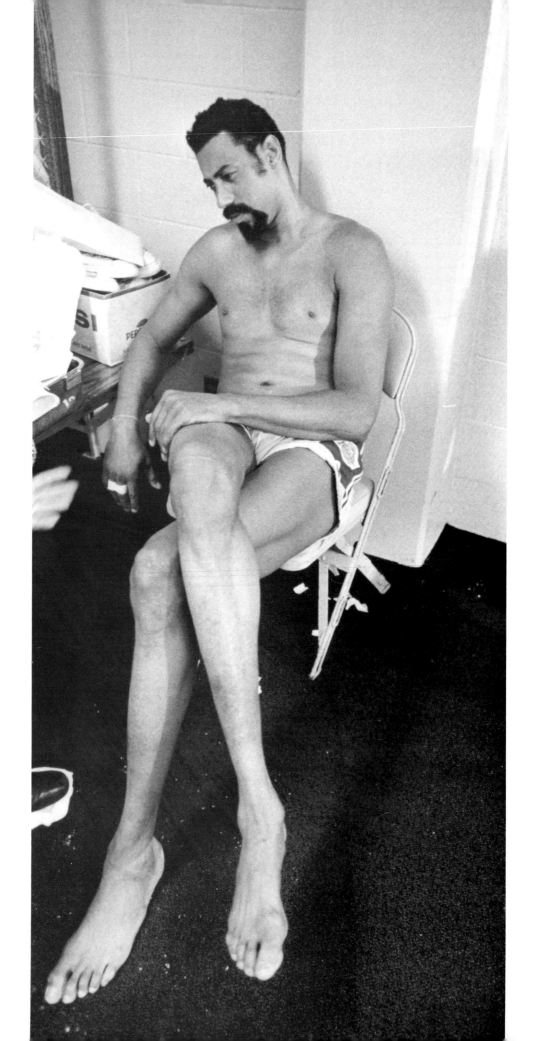

have rituals. They sit for a time and then talk to a trainer, or a ball boy, or an equipment manager. It all adds up to getting their concentration to where they feel they can perform at the ultimate level. I have the opportunity to be there and I treat it as a privilege. Some moments may be too private to photograph. People have to have confidence in me that I would never embarrass or humiliate them. I'm seeing personalities as they are seldom seen, and it's private."

Behind the scenes, George takes a unique and very personal approach. He's constantly aware of history and context. Many of the players and performers he shoots are friends, people he's known since the beginnings of their careers, when they only dreamed of greatness.

"This perspective makes me always see the hard work, the struggle, the sweat, the determination, the drive, the desire, and the character. There have been performers I've met when they were just starting out that I've always hoped would make it. As people they're very special to me, and I root for them to succeed, like family."

Photographing behind the scenes takes the thoughtful application of instinct and skill. It is anticipating a human drama long before the conflict has reached its conclusion. At its deepest level, it's about knowing people.

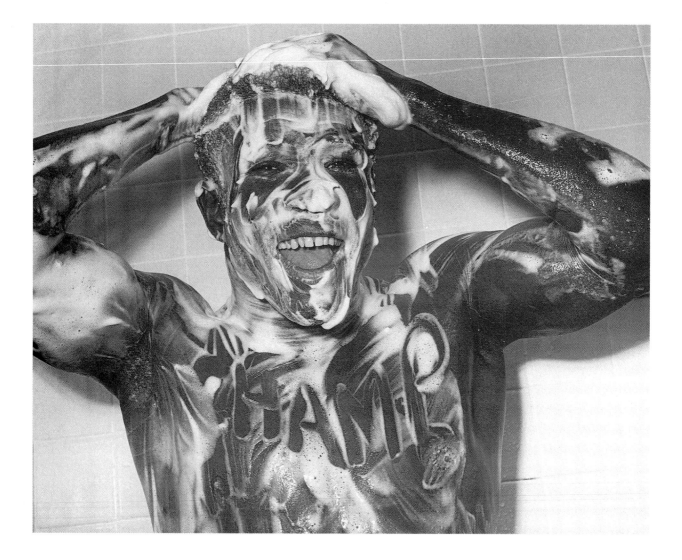

LEFT

The Empire Cat Show, 1972.

ABOVE

Backstage at the circus, 1971.

ABOVE RIGHT

A newborn donkey with its
mother after being delivered
backstage at the Garden, 1971.

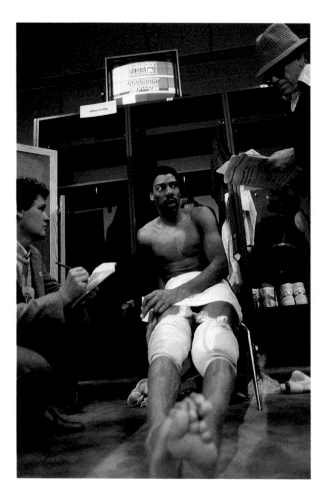

LEFT

Julius Erving after the NBA all-star game, 1985.

ABOVE

Phil Jackson in the Knicks' locker room, 1973.

RIGHT

Buster Mathis in training to fight Joe Frazier, 1968.

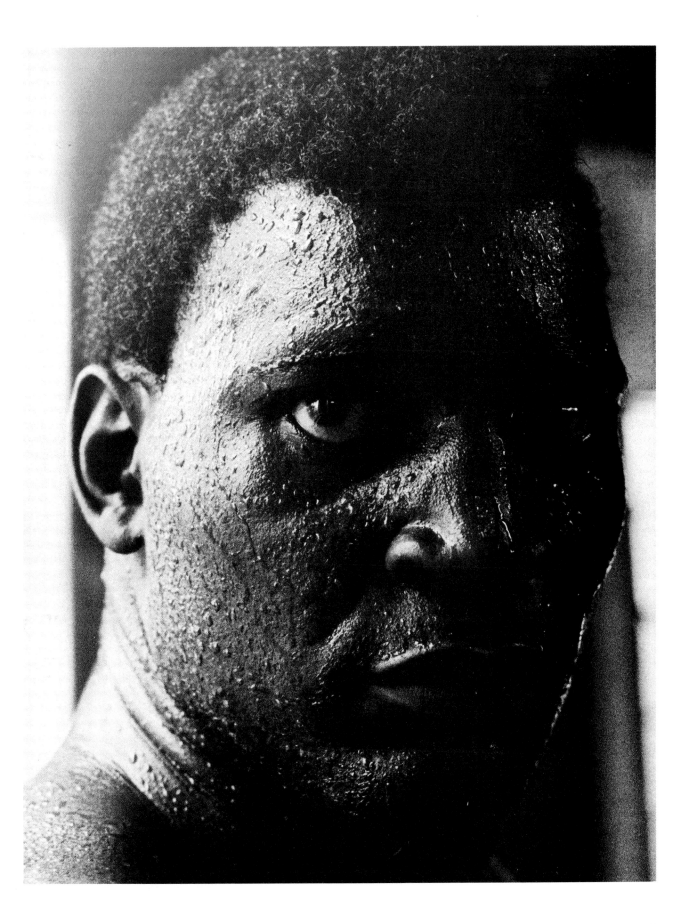

ABOVE
Walter Cronkite at the
Democratic National
Convention, 1976.

LEFT
Mark Messier, 1992.

RIGHT
Floyd Patterson in training to
fight Muhammad Ali, 1972.

FOLLOWING LEFT PAGE
Rick Barry and his son Drew,
1975.

FOLLOWING RIGHT PAGE
John Vanbiesbrouck, 1987.

THE BEST SEAT IN THE HOUSE

As far as I'm concerned," George says with an appreciative smile, "I've had the best seat in the house for over twenty-five years."

Every one of the twenty thousand seats in the Garden, or the fifty-six hundred in the Paramount, allows its occupant to be a part of the show. Fans can help the home team win or bring out the best in a singer. They heckle and cajole or send love and support. Dreams unfold before them. "A youngster goes to see what he can be," George observes. "An adult comes to see what could have been."

For many, going to the Garden is a way of life passed down from generation to generation. Some, like Freddie Klein and George Lois, have been season subscribers for thirty years. Stan Asofsky, an ardent fan for more than three decades, said, "The Garden is where we come to see excellence. Perfection. The game played the way it should be. And when it's played correctly, it's an elegant ballet, the zenith of art."

The fans have always been as big a part of Garden events as

Geese Ausby and Curly Neal of the Harlem Globetrotters, 1981.

the performers. "Certain fans can affect the outcome of a game by several points. They're sometimes more of a show than the event itself. At rock concerts or at wrestling matches, fans come dressed like the stars. Seven- and eight-year-old kids can see their heroes come to life here." Hockey superstar Brett Hull claims that hearing twenty thousand cheering for you is the greatest feeling in the world.

Fans have their own trends and fashions. The crowds at Knicks and Rangers games come dressed in the latest designer outfits. The high-fashion tennis crowd eats strawberries and sips champagne. Kids at the circus eat peanuts and cotton candy beside proud parents who feel nostalgic remembering their own first circus experience.

George often goes into the stands to capture an event. He shares the audience's excitement and learns what matters to them. "I'm looking for the same things that I look for in a performer: character, emotions, the response to the performance and the performer. The fans are tremendously varied and exciting." Sometimes, the crowd gets so animated it becomes the show and generates its own electricity. Fuzzy Levane, who has been part of the Garden for sixty years as a legendary player, coach, and scout, said warmly, "Fans at the Garden are always good, always knowledgeable and fair. If you play good, you'll hear about it. If you play lousy, believe me, you'll hear about that, too."

LEFT

Muhammad Ali finally meets his match, 1967.

ABOVE

Vanderbilt cheerleader, 1990.

RIGHT

A young fan of the Ringling Brothers and Barnum & Bailey Circus, 1968.

TOP LEFT

The Garden faithful jump for joy, 1973.

BOTTOM LEFT

Robert Klein at a Knicks game, 1990.

TOP RIGHT

Even the celebrities in the front row get into the action at the Knicks' games.

BOTTOM RIGHT

Woody Allen and Mia Farrow, 1982.

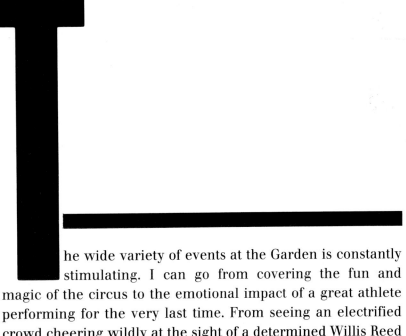

FROM THE LENS OF
GEORGE KALINSKY

The wide variety of events at the Garden is constantly stimulating. I can go from covering the fun and magic of the circus to the emotional impact of a great athlete performing for the very last time. From seeing an electrified crowd cheering wildly at the sight of a determined Willis Reed walking onto the court for the 1970 playoffs to seeing one up on its feet screaming for Pavarotti's encore, every event has an emotional impact on me, feelings that last a lifetime.

Each photograph in this section has a personal story behind it. The images reflect either an important moment in my life or a personal theme sustained over many years. One cold winter afternoon I shot an Alvin Ailey dance performance at City Center in the afternoon, an opening gala starring Mikhail Baryshnikov and Judith Jamison, and then went to the Garden for a Knick game. It occurred to me that I was really seeing the same things in both events, no matter how different some people believe them to be. There was movement, choreography, sweat, pride, pain, and endurance, the drive for excellence and the desire for perfection. Underneath it all were the same shapes and forms, united by the same themes. Each body strove to transcend itself, to achieve a unique freedom of spirit and victory. Whether scoring a point or executing a leap, here was the drama of human endeavor exemplified by awesome effort. These elements are in every good image. The common thread.

One of my favorite pictures, one that is always being requested, is the sad clown character of the Ringling Brothers circus. One afternoon, I happened to wander into the arena near the end of a circus performance. I was close to where the clown was sitting as he was doing his knitting act. I'd known him for a few years, but for some reason this day he looked especially sad, sadder than I'd ever seen him. His mouth seemed to tremble. His eyes held fear. He was not acting. The sadness in his face touched me and I felt compelled to take a picture of him.

I followed him back to his dressing room. As I spoke to him, he seemed to be looking into space. He took off his jacket and picked up several newspapers, making a pillow of them. Then he lay down on a bench against the wall. He looked at me, and I saw he was afraid. I tried to comfort him as best I could, and he fell asleep with his greasepaint still on his face. He never woke up. The next morning every New York newspaper carried the story of his death from throat cancer. This man who made us laugh, who made millions of people feel so good, died alone on a bench near twenty thousand empty seats. Circus people will tell you he was the greatest clown who ever lived. His name was Otto Griebling.

The image of Muhammad Ali is significant because he remained an important part of my life and my career. He is probably the most enjoyable personality I have ever photographed. In September 1976, a few weeks before he was to defeat Ken Norton in a Garden promotion at Yankee Stadium, I went out at four thirty in the morning to photograph Ali doing roadwork at his training camp at the Concord Hotel in the Catskills. After the roadwork photos, Ali went to his room to rest. A few hours later I brought my wife, Ellen, with me to his room to chat. Ali, always a showman in public, spoke very softly in private, sometimes just a whisper. He acknowledged, for the first time, in a soft, sincere voice, that his best days were behind him and that Ken Norton was a good fighter. Ellen asked him why he didn't give up fighting. "I keep fighting," Ali said, "because I'm afraid to stop. If I stop the world will forget me. People won't

recognize me as much. I got to be in front of the public. I'm no doctor, I'm no lawyer—but I realize now I must prepare for the future. I must read more. I know I must write. I need to speak my mind. Right now the ring is my stage. Boxing is only a means to be in the public eye. I am recognized all over the world, but that is now, and because I'm still in the ring—I know that." Then Ali sat up in bed and said to Ellen, as he made a fist and a mock-mean face, "Make sure this guy takes good care of you, because he'll be hearing from me if he don't."

Of all the athletes I've photographed or known personally, Willis Reed is the exemplar of the will to win. No one ever gave the game or his teammates more of himself. One of the greatest moments in sports I've ever seen was when Willis came onto the court after being injured in the play-offs. I don't think there's ever been a bigger crowd reaction. My photographs of some of the Garden's legendary moments are on the walls outside the dressing rooms. Magic Johnson recently walked out of the locker room and happened to see the photo of Willis Reed that appears in this section. He stopped, studied the expression on Willis's face for a while, and said knowingly, "That's what it's all about."

I visited the Vietnam Veterans Memorial in Washington, the wall of names, to find my cousin's. It was raining lightly as I looked at the impressive memorial statue of the three soldiers in combat. One face seemed to come to life before my eyes. The rain created the effect of mud and sweat on the soldier's face, as if he had just come in from the battlefield. The lifeless stone face seemed to be breathing. The soldier had the same look of pride, strength, and determination that I have seen on the faces of Muhammad Ali, Willis Reed, Emile Griffith, and so many other athletes I have photographed in the heat of battle at the Garden. It is for that reason that it is paired here with the sweaty visage of Emile Griffith, himself a study of inner determination and strength.

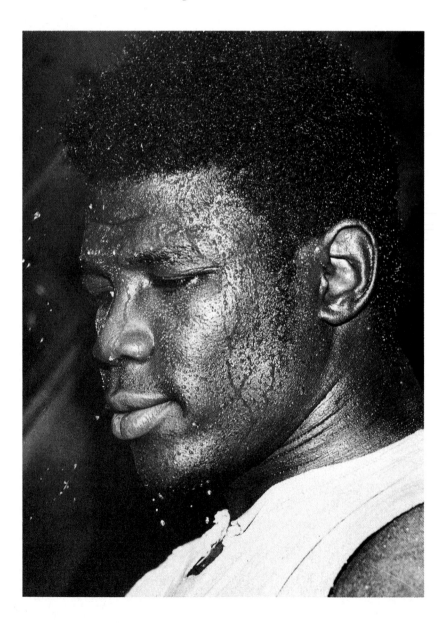

Family and sports have certainly been two of the most important influences in my life. Success requires support and assistance. My wife, Ellen, and I have shared most of life's trials and errors. Not only has our love grown, but Ellen is—and always will be—my best friend. Photographing and meeting so many wonderful people at the Garden was a privilege I wanted to share with my family. "Dad, can I go to the Garden? Dad, can I use your camera and take pictures?" How many times did I hear those questions from my two children, Lee and Rachelle? I was always thrilled to bring them. For many of the events I have photographed, they have been my assistants. If I grew up in the Garden, then they grew up with me. They're both excellent photographers and loyal assistants. When I need them, they are always there, always willing to give of themselves.

The photograph of the Harlem Magicians was taken during the final night of basketball in the old Garden. Former Globetrotter Marques Haynes, known as the world's greatest dribbler, had formed his own team, the Harlem Magicians, and they played at the Garden as part of the doubleheaders. When I was still an art director, I met Marques at the Garden, told him that I loved his playing, and showed him how I tried to imitate his dribbling routine. In two weeks I found myself playing on the Magicians, filling in for Marques for a few minutes here and there. It was such a thrill for me. When I took the

photograph, I remembered the legends and the great teams that played the Garden. I also remembered the years of my relationship with Marques. The picture was taken as the game got down to the final seconds. Marques grabbed my five-year-old son, Lee, brought him onto the court, gave him the ball, and lifted him up to the basket so he could score the final basket as the buzzer sounded.

The photo featuring John Condon was taken on 125th Street in Harlem, during a publicity bout he staged to publicize an upcoming fight between lightweight champ Carlos Ortiz and Ismael Laguna outdoors at Shea Stadium in 1967. Condon loved to set up the actual Garden ring all over New York City to promote boxing. He wanted to bring boxing to the people, to get them close to it, so he went right into the city's diverse neighborhoods with the famous ring. He staged events in front of the Plaza, in Times Square, in Brooklyn—he even did one on top of the Garden marquee. He was a truly great promoter, a real lover of the sport.

John promoted the Ortiz fight with the press, telling everyone that Ortiz was going to spar outside on Saturday afternoon. Unfortunately, he didn't bother with the necessary permits. He had called somebody who probably said he had to go down to City Hall and get permits for the sound truck, the music, the extra police, and so on. But John didn't worry about that. He just went ahead.

There was a big crowd. We had buckets and pails and stools and lots of equipment all brought over in a minibus. A police lieutenant demanded to see the street permits for the event. John suddenly "remembered" he left them at his Garden office. He called over one Mushky McGee, and told the policeman he would send his "trusted lieutenant" to get them. The police lieutenant left. John gave Mushky twenty dollars, told him to have an early dinner at Gallagher's and go home. John began the event. He spoke. An assemblyman spoke. The police lieutenant came back with a captain.

This time John sent Sam Graham "to get the permits." Sam was about seventy. John said, "Here's twenty bucks. Go have dinner and don't come back." Half an hour later, the captain and the lieutenant were ready to explode. They told John if they didn't see the permits they were going to close him down in twenty minutes. John was at a loss, and Tom Kenville, who worked closely with John, was wondering whom to call to forestall the shutdown, when all of a sudden a loud siren blared and a huge black limo pulled to a stop. It was Mayor Lindsay. He had promised John he'd be a guest referee for three rounds. We didn't hear another word about permits. All the cops wanted their pictures taken. Lindsay stayed and the day was a total success. Condon's only comment as they were packing up later was "What the heck were you all so worried about?"

The next day, the front page of the Sunday *New York Times* carried the picture of Mayor Lindsay refereeing the Ortiz bout.

On April 26, 1990, Madison Square Garden was the site of a special celebration honoring the ninth completion of the Talmud, the book of Jewish law and guidelines. Twenty thousand Orthodox Jews came for this historic religious event, the largest gathering of its kind in American Jewish history. In preparation for the event, Ellen and I went to the Lower East Side to visit several Orthodox establishments, one a store selling religious artifacts. In the back of the store I saw a rabbi (scribe) proofreading and hand-printing the sacred scroll called the Torah. In a moment that had special spiritual meaning for me, the rabbi gave me permission to photograph him performing the three-thousand-year-old sacred ritual.

All of a sudden something came alive for me, a direct connection to the history and traditions of my people. I had never seen anything like this before. In touching the sacred books, those wonderful hands were reaching back to the original scrolls that were handed to Moses. Being Jewish and knowing about Jewish history, I felt a link to people and events that took place thousands of years ago. It moved me deeply.

One of my most memorable photo opportunities was during Pope John Paul II's visit to the Garden. While twenty thousand people awaited the pontiff's arrival, I was waiting backstage with the Garden's welcoming representatives. The pope's limo came up the ramp. I was the only one with a camera. The door opened in front of me and the pope came out, smiling. He looked at me and made an incredible spiritual impression. I started clicking away while the Garden staff greeted him, and then proceeded to the arena stands to find a place to shoot from. There were 250 other photographers around, but I was determined to get the best picture. Luck was to play a key role.

The pope's car entered the arena, bringing his wonderful glowing smile to the joyous crowd. Then, suddenly, the pope was in front of me again. The crowd became silent and hushed as he picked up a little girl—who was standing right next to me. He held her up for a few seconds and looked at her as she looked at him. With all the thousands of people at the Garden that day, he could not have known he was selecting a child whose father, a New York City detective, had been shot and killed only weeks before. Despite the commotion of the Garden and the millions of TV viewers watching her awed face, she looked deeply into his warm and consoling eyes. It was a private moment, one that crystallized the simple personal emotions that people bring to complex events. My photo was